Canadian Money Activities: Teacher Tips

Depending on the experience of the students introduce different coins or bills daily. Play,"What am I?"
Give students hints about what coin or bill you are talking about. Then students have to guess the coin or bill.

Use coins to count daily to the 100th day of school. Start with a penny and trade up to a nickel,
dime, quarter, etc., until the class reaches a loonie to represent 100th day.

Create a class store: Have students bring in different packages, empty products, menus or store flyers for the
students to "buy" in the store. Label and price items using stickers or index cards. Assign students as customers
who will "buy" items from the store and students who will act as cashiers who "sell" in the store. Before customers
go shopping give them a set amount of money to spend. Use notebooks to keep track of purchases and change.

Practice money math problems and exercises including addition, subtraction, and comparing values.
Create a daily money question. Ask students questions such as:

- How much each coin/bill or other amount of money is worth.

- What coin/bill or other amount of money has the greatest value.

- How much money they would have if they had one penny, one nickel, and one dime or other combinations.

Use the blackline masters at the back of this book to create your own worksheets for your students.

Other Extensions:

Have students write journals about money. Some journal topics might include:

- How is money used in our daily lives?

- If I had a million dollars...

- Would you want to work in a bank? Why or why not?

Have someone from a local bank come for a class visit to talk to the students about banks, opening accounts,
and keeping track of deposits and withdrawals.

Have students visit the following website to play *Change Maker* to practice money skills:

http://www.funbrain.com/cashreg

Canadian Money Activities 1-4

Get To Know Canadian Coins

A. Match the correct value to each coin.

1.

$ 1. 00

2.

$ 0. 05

3.

$ 0. 01

4.

$ 2. 00

5.

$ 0. 10

6.

$ 0. 25

B. Write the following coin amount in cents.

7. $ 0. 10 _____

8. $ 0. 25 _____

9. $ 0. 05 _____

10. $ 0. 01 _____

Chalkboard Publishing Inc © 2007

Get to Know Canadian Coins

A. **C**ut and paste the money words to match the coins.

penny	quarter	toonie
nickel	dime	loonie

Chalkboard Publishing Inc © 2007

Get To Know Canadian Coins

A. **C**ut and paste the coins to match the descriptions.

1.
This is a penny.
1¢ $0.01

2.
This is a nickel.
5¢ $0.05

3.
This is a dime.
10¢ $0.10

4.
This is a quarter.
25¢ $0.25

5.
This is a loonie.
100¢ $1.00

6.
This is a toonie.
200¢ $2.00

Chalkboard Publishing Inc © 2007

Get to Know Canadian Coins

A. Circle the pennies RED. Circle the dimes BLUE. Circle the nickels YELLOW. Circle the quarters GREEN.

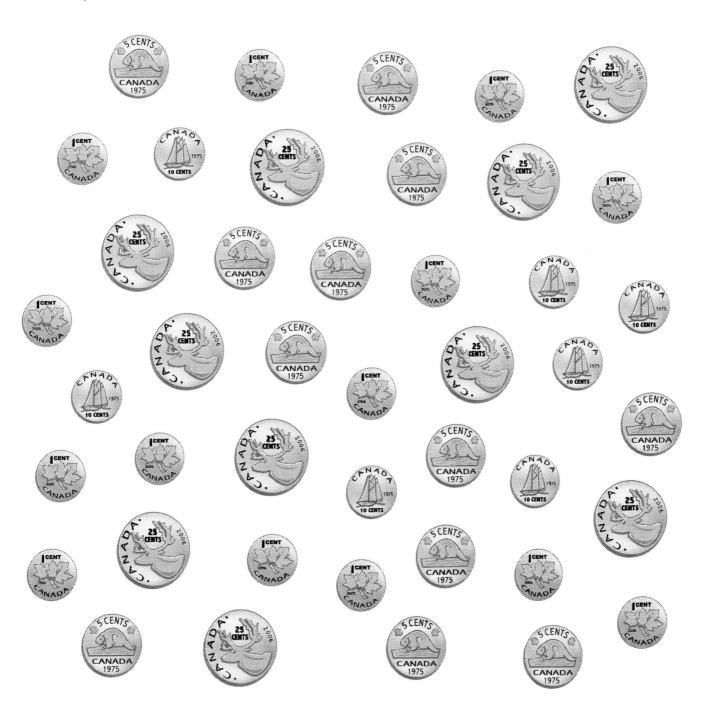

B. Brain Stretch: Write the amount of money in decimal form.

1. **How many pennies?** _____

2. **How many quarters?** _____

3. **How many dimes?** _____

4. **How many nickels?** _____

Canadian Money Activities 1-4

Counting Pennies

A. **C**ount on by 1's to find the value of the pennies.

1.

_____¢   _____¢   _____¢   _____¢   _____¢   =   _____¢

2.

_____¢   _____¢   _____¢   =   _____¢

3.

_____¢   _____¢   _____¢   _____¢   _____¢   _____¢   =   _____¢

4.

_____¢   _____¢   _____¢   _____¢   =   _____¢

5.

_____¢   _____¢   _____¢   _____¢   _____¢   _____¢   _____¢   =   _____¢

Chalkboard Publishing Inc © 2007

Canadian Money Activities 1-4

Counting Nickels

A. **C**ount on by 5's to find the value of the nickels.

1.

_____ ¢   _____ ¢   _____ ¢   _____ ¢   _____ ¢   =   _____ ¢

2.

_____ ¢   _____ ¢   _____ ¢   =   _____ ¢

3.

_____ ¢   _____ ¢   _____ ¢   _____ ¢   _____ ¢   _____ ¢   =   _____ ¢

4.

_____ ¢   _____ ¢   _____ ¢   _____ ¢   =   _____ ¢

5.

_____ ¢   _____ ¢   _____ ¢   _____ ¢   _____ ¢   _____ ¢   _____ ¢   =   _____ ¢

Canadian Money Activities 1-4

Counting Dimes

10 CENTS

A. Count on by 10's to find the value of the dimes.

1.

_____ ¢   _____ ¢   _____ ¢   _____ ¢   _____ ¢   =   _____ ¢

2.

_____ ¢   _____ ¢   _____ ¢   =   _____ ¢

3.

_____ ¢   _____ ¢   _____ ¢   _____ ¢   _____ ¢   _____ ¢   =   _____ ¢

4.

_____ ¢   _____ ¢   _____ ¢   _____ ¢   =   _____ ¢

5.

_____ ¢   _____ ¢   _____ ¢   _____ ¢   _____ ¢   _____ ¢   _____ ¢   =   _____ ¢

     Canadian Money Activities 1-4

Counting Nickels and Pennies

A. To find the value of the coins: count by 5's for nickels and count by 1's for pennies.

_____ ¢   _____ ¢   _____ ¢   _____ ¢   _____ ¢   =   _____ ¢

_____ ¢   _____ ¢   _____ ¢   _____ ¢   _____ ¢   =   _____ ¢

_____ ¢   _____ ¢   _____ ¢   _____ ¢   _____ ¢   =   _____ ¢

_____ ¢   _____ ¢   _____ ¢   _____ ¢   =   _____ ¢

_____ ¢   _____ ¢   _____ ¢   _____ ¢   _____ ¢   =   _____ ¢

Canadian Money Activities 1-4

Counting Dimes and Nickels

A. **T**o find the value of the coins: count by 5's for nickels and count by 10's for dimes.

1.

_____ ¢   _____ ¢   _____ ¢   _____ ¢   _____ ¢   _____ ¢   _____ ¢ = _____ ¢

2.

_____ ¢   _____ ¢   _____ ¢   _____ ¢   _____ ¢   _____ ¢   _____ ¢ = _____ ¢

3.

_____ ¢   _____ ¢   _____ ¢   _____ ¢   _____ ¢   _____ ¢   _____ ¢ = _____ ¢

4.

_____ ¢   _____ ¢   _____ ¢   _____ ¢   _____ ¢   _____ ¢   _____ ¢ = _____ ¢

5.

_____ ¢   _____ ¢   _____ ¢   _____ ¢   _____ ¢   _____ ¢   _____ ¢ = _____ ¢

Canadian Money Activities 1-4

Counting Dimes, Nickels and Pennies

A. To find the value of the coins: count by 10's for dimes, count by 5's for nickels and count by 1's for pennies.

1.

_____ ¢ _____ ¢ _____ ¢ _____ ¢ _____ ¢ _____ ¢ _____ ¢ = _____ ¢

2.

_____ ¢ _____ ¢ _____ ¢ _____ ¢ _____ ¢ _____ ¢ _____ ¢ = _____ ¢

3.

_____ ¢ _____ ¢ _____ ¢ _____ ¢ _____ ¢ _____ ¢ _____ ¢ = _____ ¢

4.

_____ ¢ _____ ¢ _____ ¢ _____ ¢ _____ ¢ _____ ¢ _____ ¢ = _____ ¢

5.

_____ ¢ _____ ¢ _____ ¢ _____ ¢ _____ ¢ _____ ¢ _____ ¢ = _____ ¢

Canadian Money Activities 1-4

Counting Coins

1.

_____ ¢ _____ ¢ _____ ¢ _____ ¢ _____ ¢ _____ ¢ _____ ¢ = _____ ¢

2.

_____ ¢ _____ ¢ _____ ¢ _____ ¢ _____ ¢ _____ ¢ _____ ¢ = _____ ¢

3.

_____ ¢ _____ ¢ _____ ¢ _____ ¢ _____ ¢ _____ ¢ _____ ¢ = _____ ¢

4.

_____ ¢ _____ ¢ _____ ¢ _____ ¢ _____ ¢ _____ ¢ _____ ¢ = _____ ¢

5.

_____ ¢ _____ ¢ _____ ¢ _____ ¢ _____ ¢ _____ ¢ _____ ¢ = _____ ¢

(12)

Counting Coins

A. **What is the value of each amount of coins?**

1.

2.

3.

4.

5.

6.

7.

8.

9.

10.

Canadian Money Activities 1-4

Coin Addition

1. **+** = _____ ¢

2.   **+**   = _____ ¢

3.   **+**   = _____ ¢

4. **+**   = _____ ¢

5. **+** = _____ ¢

Coin Addition

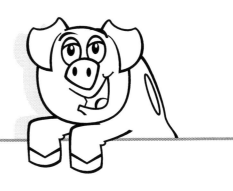

A. **Add the coins.**

1. **+**   = _____ ¢

2.   **+** = _____ ¢

3.   **+**   = _____ ¢

4.   **+** = _____ ¢

5.   **+** = _____ ¢

Canadian Money Activities 1-4

Coin Subtraction

A. Subtract the coins.

1.

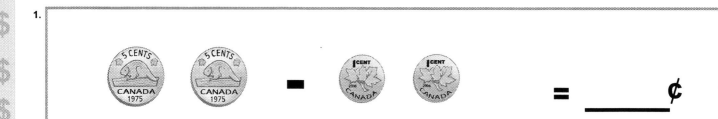

= _____ ¢

2.

= _____ ¢

3.

= _____ ¢

4.

= _____ ¢

5.

= _____ ¢

Chalkboard Publishing Inc © 2007

Canadian Money Activities 1-4

At the Post Office

A. Caroline is mailing a letter. She needs 60 ¢ worth of stamps. What stamps could she use?

B. Rob is mailing a package. He needs 35 ¢ worth of stamps. What stamps can he use?

C. Mike is mailing a package. He needs 45 ¢ worth of stamps. What stamps can he use?

Chalkboard Publishing Inc © 2007

Canadian Money Activities 1-4

What are the Coins?

A. Circle the coins that match the price.

1.
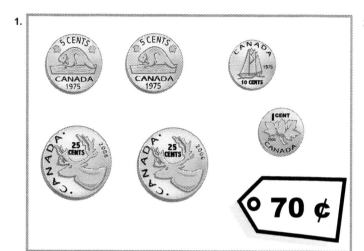

2.
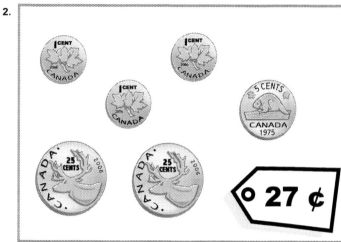

3.

4.
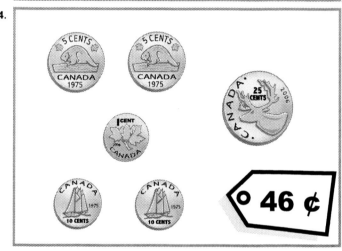

5.
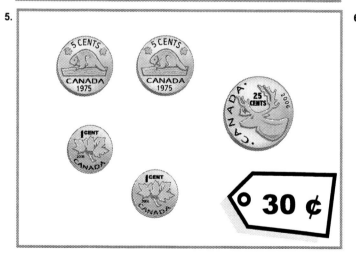

6.
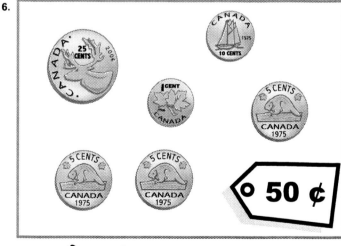

Chalkboard Publishing Inc © 2007

Canadian Money Activities 1-4

Money Match

○ $0.41
○ $1.00
○ $0.93
○ $0.61
○ $0.52
○ $0.39

Canadian Money Activities 1-4

Show the Money!

A. Show the correct amount of coins for each coin value.

1.

○ 32 ¢

2.

○ 67 ¢

3.

○ 51 ¢

4.

○ 24 ¢

5.

○ 78 ¢

6.

○ 45 ¢

Canadian Money Activities 1-4

Show the Money!

A. Show the correct amount of coins for each coin value.

1.

○ **80 ¢**

2.

○ **79 ¢**

3.

○ **56 ¢**

4.

○ **93 ¢**

5.

○ **62 ¢**

6.

○ **23 ¢**

Canadian Money Activities 1-4

Let's make $1.00

A. Show different ways to make $ 1.00.

1.

2.

3.

4.

5.

6.

Canadian Money Activities 1-4

Coin Addition

A. **Add the coins.**

Show your work.

1.

+
= _____ ¢

2.

+
= _____ ¢

3.

+
= _____ ¢

4.

+

= _____ ¢

5.

+

= _____ ¢

Chalkboard Publishing Inc © 2007

Canadian Money Activities 1-4

Coin Addition

A. Add the coins.

1.

+ = _____ ¢

2.

+   = _____ ¢

3.

+   = _____ ¢

4.

+   = _____ ¢

5.

+  = _____ ¢

Canadian Money Activities 1-4

Coin Subtraction

A. **Subtract the coins.**

Show your work.

1.
 − 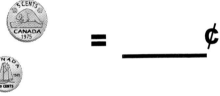 = _____ ¢

2.
 −  = _____ ¢

3.
 −  = _____ ¢

4.
 −  = _____ ¢

5.
 −   = _____ ¢

25

Coin Subtraction

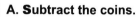

A. Subtract the coins.

Show your work.

1.

= _____ ¢

2.

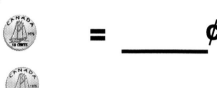

= _____ ¢

3.

= _____ ¢

4.

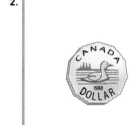 

= _____ ¢

5.

= _____ ¢

26

Find the Coins

A. Count and draw to find the coins.

1.
Draw 27 ¢ using 5 coins.

2.
Draw 40 ¢ using 3 coins.

3.
Draw 24 ¢ using 6 coins.

4.
Draw 82 ¢ using 6 coins.

5.
Draw 61 ¢ using 4 coins.

6.
Draw 18 ¢ using 6 coins.

Canadian Money Activities 1-4

Fewest Number of Coins

A. Show each amount by using the fewest number of coins.

1. **27¢** _____ _____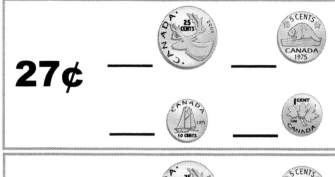
   _____ _____

2. **59¢** _____ _____
   _____ _____

3. **48¢** _____ _____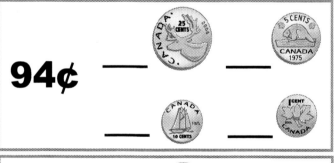
   _____ _____

4. **36¢** _____ _____
   _____ _____

5. **63¢** _____ _____
   _____ _____

6. **90¢** _____ _____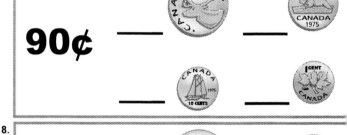
   _____ _____

7. **94¢** _____ _____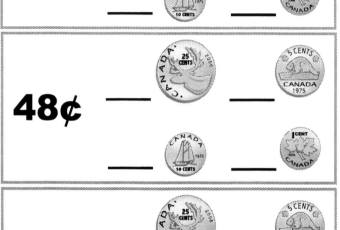
   _____ _____

8. **80¢** _____ _____
   _____ _____

9. **41¢** _____ _____
   _____ _____

10. **75¢** _____ _____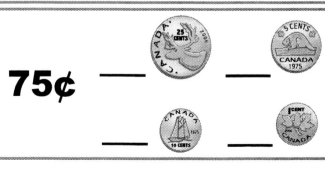
    _____ _____

Canadian Money Activities 1-4

Equal Amounts

A. Show two ways to make equal amounts.

First Way	Second Way

1. 83¢

2. 90¢

3. 75¢

4. 29¢

5. 38¢

Equal Amounts

A. **S**how two ways to make equal amounts.

First Way   **Second Way**

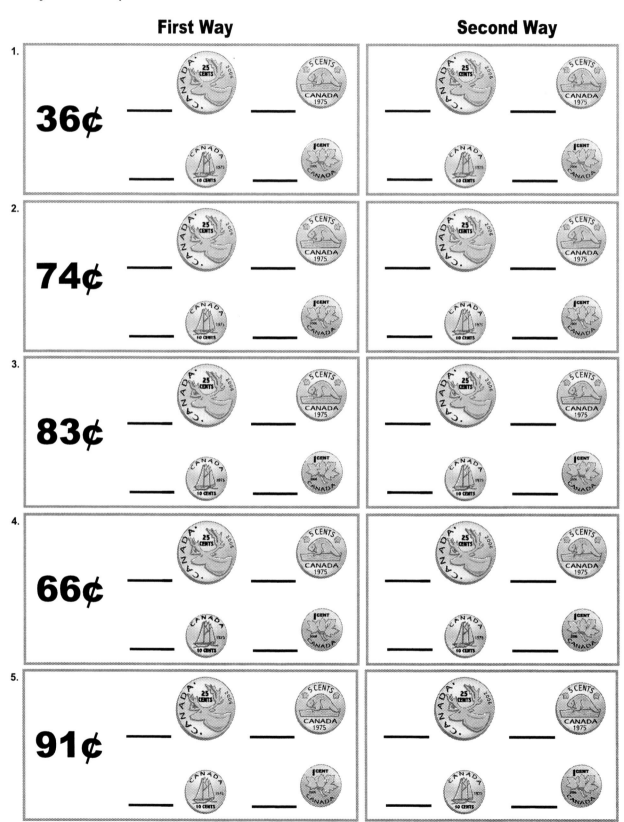

Chalkboard Publishing Inc © 2007

Show the Money!

A. Cut and paste or draw the correct amount of coins.

1.

○ $2.35

2.

○ $1.43

3.

○ $5.90

4.

○ $4.10

5.

○ $3.76

6.

○ $8.16

Show the Money!

A. **C**ut and paste or draw the correct amount of coins.

1.

◦ **$6.18**

2.

◦ **$7.16**

3.

◦ **$5.20**

4.

◦ **$4.23**

5.

◦ **$3.54**

6.

◦ **$7.82**

Chalkboard Publishing Inc © 2007

Canadian Money Activities 1-4

Missing Coins

A. Fill in the missing coin value.

1.

   1 quarter   +   8 nickels   +   4 pennies   = _____ ¢

2.

   2 quarters   +   4 dimes   +   _____ pennies   =   97 ¢

3.

   3 dimes   +   _____ nickels   +   8 pennies   =   88 ¢

4.

   _____ quarter   +   5 nickels   +   7 pennies   +   1 dime   =   67 ¢

5.

   _____ quarters   +   4 nickels   +   9 pennies   =   79 ¢

6.

   2 quarters   +   6 nickels   +   _____ pennies   =   80 ¢

7.

   8 nickels   +   5 dimes   +   _____ pennies   =   97 ¢

8.

   2 quarters   +   2 nickels   +   1 dime   +   5 pennies   = _____ ¢

Chalkboard Publishing Inc © 2007

Canadian Money Activities 1-4

Fewest Coins

A. **Draw the fewest coins to show the following amounts.**

1.
> **Draw $2.20 using 5 coins.**

2.
> **Draw $5.44 using 12 coins.**

3.
> **Draw $2.84 using 9 coins.**

4.
> **Draw $4.57 using 9 coins.**

5.
> **Draw $8.82 using 11 coins.**

Canadian Money Activities 1-4

At the Snack Bar

A. Answer the following questions.

Chips  **$0.25**

Chocolate Bar  **$0.33**

Drink **$0.46**

Ice Cream Bar 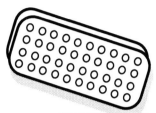 **$0.52**

1. What is the price of a drink and a chocolate bar?

2. What is the price of chips and an ice cream bar?

3. What is the price of an ice cream and a drink.

4. How much do two drinks cost?

5. You buy a drink and pay with a loonie. What is your change?

6. You buy an ice cream bar and pay with a loonie. What is your change?

Chalkboard Publishing Inc © 2007

Canadian Money Activities 1-4

At the School Cafeteria

A. Menu.

Pizza Slice  **$1.50**

Sandwich **$1.90**

Macaroni and Cheese **$1.80**

Veggie Sticks **$1.15**

Juice **$0.85**

Chocolate Milk **$0.90**

Lemonade  **$0.95**

Jello **$0.85**

36

At the School Cafeteria

A. Answer the following questions.

---

1. Write the prices of the items on the cafeteria menu from least to greatest.

Juice, Jello, Chocolate milk, lemonade, veggie sticks, Pizza, Macaroni and cheese, Sandwich

---

2. How much are 2 pizza slices and 1 veggie sticks?

$14.15

$$
\begin{array}{r}
1.50 \\
+1.50 \\
+1.15 \\
\hline
4.15
\end{array}
$$

---

3. How much is a pizza slice, veggie sticks and a chocolate milk?

$3.55

$$
\begin{array}{r}
1.50 \\
+1.15 \\
0.90 \\
\hline
3.55
\end{array}
$$

---

4. Tenzin bought a sandwich. She paid with a toonie. What is her change?

$0.04

---

5. How much is 1 macaroni and cheese, and 1 juice? If David gives the cashier 2 toonies, is it enough money? Explain.

$$
\begin{array}{r}
1.80 \\
+0.85 \\
\hline
2.65
\end{array}
\qquad
\begin{array}{r}
4.00 \\
-2.65 \\
\hline
1.35
\end{array}
$$

It is enough because they both together or $2.65 but two toonies is $4.00. His change is $1.35.

Chalkboard Publishing Inc © 2007

At the School Cafeteria

A. **A**nswer the following questions.

1. How much is a 1 pizza slice, 1 juice and 1 jello? If Jane gives the cashier 1 loonie and 1 toonie, does she have enough money to pay? Explain.

2. Dara has $5.00 to buy lunch for her and her little brother. What can she buy for lunch for both of them?

3. Michael has $4.00. He buys 1 sandwich, and 1 lemonade. Does he have enough money for a jello? Explain.

4. What would you buy at the cafeteria if you had 3 toonies?

5. What would you buy at the cafeteria if you had $10.00?

Chalkboard Publishing Inc © 2007

Canadian Money Activities 1-4

Comparing Money Values

A. Compare and write >, < or = in the ◯ .

1.
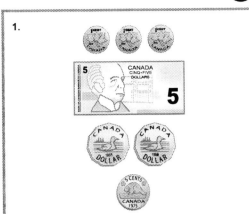

◯

What is the value? _____   What is the value? _____

2.

◯

What is the value? _____   What is the value? _____

3.

◯

What is the value? _____   What is the value? _____

B. Brain Stretch: Write each amount of money in decimal form.

1. twelve dollars and nine cents _____

2. forty-four dollars and six cents _____

3. nine dollars and fourty four cents _____

Canadian Money Activities 1-4

Comparing Money Values

A. Compare and write >, < or = in the ⭕ .

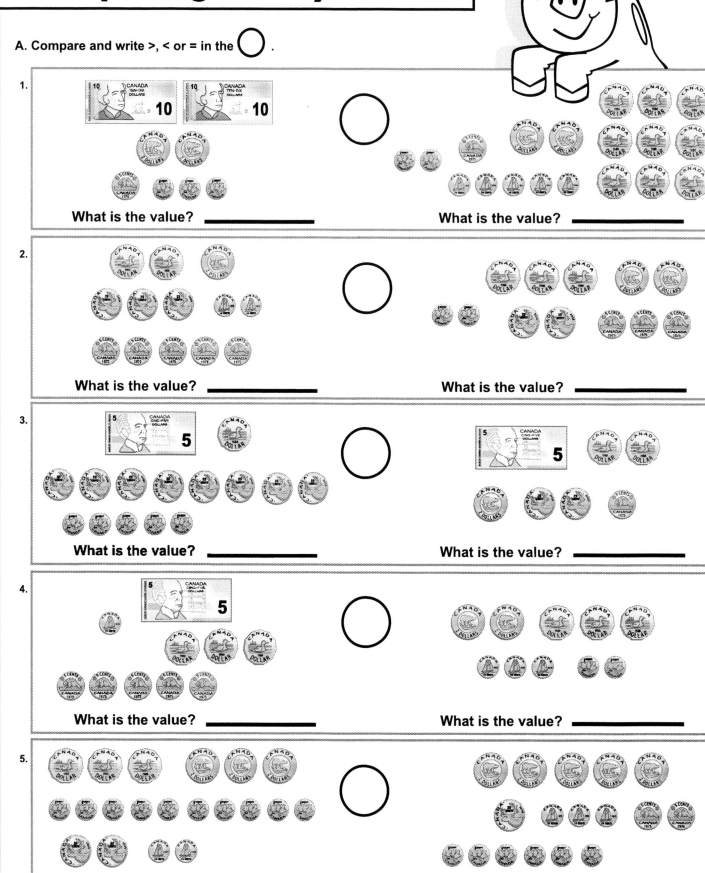

1. What is the value? _____   What is the value? _____

2. What is the value? _____   What is the value? _____

3. What is the value? _____   What is the value? _____

4. What is the value? _____   What is the value? _____

5. What is the value? _____   What is the value? _____

Canadian Money Activities 1-4

How Much Money?

A. Count and write the value of each amount of money.

1.

2.

3.

4.

5.

Canadian Money Activities 1-4

How Much Money?

A. **Count and write the value of each amount of money.**

Show your work.

1.

2.

3.

4.

5.

42

Writing Money In Decimal Form

A. **R**ewrite each amount of money in decimal form.

2 twenty-dollar bills, 6 nickels, 2 pennies. _____	2. 1 twenty-dollar bills, 5 nickels. 4 quarters, 3 dimes _____
3 ten-dollar bills, 7 dimes, 1 nickel _____	4. 1 quarter, 9 pennies, 4 nickels _____
4 loonies, 8 dimes, 3 pennies, 3 quarters, 4 nickels _____	6. 8 pennies, 5 nickels, 2 dimes _____
4 five-dollar bills, 2 toonies, 9 nickels _____	8. 1 dime, 6 pennies _____
7 dimes, 6 quarters, 4 nickels _____	10. 5 quarters, 8 nickels _____
2 five-dollar bills, 1 loonie, 2 quarters, 1 dime _____	12. 5 toonies, 4 quarters, 5 nickels, 7 dimes _____
3 ten-dollar bills, 3 nickels, 6 dimes _____	14. 2 pennies, 9 nickels, 2 quarters, 2 loonies _____

15. 3 five-dollar bills, 3 pennies, 8 dimes, 4 nickels

_____

Chalkboard Publishing Inc © 2007

Canadian Money Activities 1-4

Writing Money In Decimal Form

A. Rewrite each amount of money in decimal form.

1. 7 dimes, 3 pennies, 5 quarters
_____

2. 3 twenty-dollar bills, 1 loonie, 5 nickels, 4 quarters, 6 pennies
_____

3. 4 twenty-dollar bills, 1 nickel, 9 dimes
_____

4. 2 twenty-dollar bills, 1 toonie, 4 dimes, 8 pennies, 1 quarter
_____

5. 2 five-dollar bills, 2 dimes, 3 nickels, 2 quarters, 6 pennies
_____

6. 9 nickels, 2 pennies, 3 quarters
_____

7. 2 ten-dollar bills, 6 five-dollar bills, 8 dimes, 5 pennies
_____

8. 1 ten-dollar bill, 6 quarters, 1 nickel, 7 pennies
_____

9. 3 ten-dollar bills, 4 pennies, 8 dimes
_____

10. 3 nickels, 4 dimes, 6 pennies
_____

11. 1 nickel, 3 quarters
_____

12. 9 toonies, 7 nickels, 9 dimes
_____

13. 4 loonies, 5 quarters, 5 pennies, 2 dimes, 3 nickels
_____

14. 7 pennies, 4 quarters, 2 nickels
_____

15. 1 fifty-dollar bill , 1 twenty-dollar bill, 4 dimes
_____

Canadian Money Activities 1-4

Rounding Money To The Nearest Dollar

A. Round to the nearest dollar.

1. $929.42 _____	2. $6.47 _____
3. $70.38 _____	4. $10.02 _____
5. $5.74 _____	6. $169.57 _____
7. $7.56 _____	8. $407.26 _____
9. $638.69 _____	10. $78.95 _____
11. $73.80 _____	12. $3.11 _____
13. $612.24 _____	14. $7.49 _____
15. $85.40 _____	16. $90.73 _____
17. $578.01 _____	18. $6.53 _____

Canadian Money Activities 1-4

Rounding Money

A. **R**ound to the place value of the underlined digit.

1. **$9**6.28

2. **$5**3.55

3. **$1.**55

4. **$4.**64

5. **$1**.76

6. **$3**6.99

7. **$9**.82

8. **$50**.10

9. **$2**6.48

10. **$7**.07

11. **$4**.31

12. **$40**.43

13. **$6**.52

14. **$34**.90

15. **$30**.68

16. **$8**.34

17. **$7**.26

18. **$2**.50

Canadian Money Activities 1-4

Comparing Money

A. Compare and write >, < or = in the $\bigcirc$.

1. $53.82 $\bigcirc$ $3.82

2. $78.25 $\bigcirc$ $25.78

3. $0.97 $\bigcirc$ $0.97

4. $34.59 $\bigcirc$ $26.59

5. $61.18 $\bigcirc$ $80.04

6. $5.35 $\bigcirc$ $5.76

7. $36.50 $\bigcirc$ $35.60

8. $2.31 $\bigcirc$ $2.57

9. $59.43 $\bigcirc$ $59.44

10. $8.01 $\bigcirc$ $8.10

11. $43.05 $\bigcirc$ $12.82

12. $6.80 $\bigcirc$ $6.44

13. $4.76 $\bigcirc$ $9.99

14. $94.53 $\bigcirc$ $94.60

15. $87.27 $\bigcirc$ $87.72

16. $7.16 $\bigcirc$ $7.61

17. $2.43 $\bigcirc$ $1.38

18. $56.74 $\bigcirc$ $56.06

Chalkboard Publishing Inc © 2007

Canadian Money Activities 1-4

Money Problems

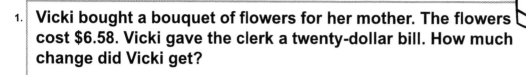

A. **S**olve the following money problems. Show your thinking.

1. Vicki bought a bouquet of flowers for her mother. The flowers cost $6.58. Vicki gave the clerk a twenty-dollar bill. How much change did Vicki get?

2. A box of Crunchy Oats cereal costs $3.84. If Michael buys a box, how much change will he get from a ten-dollar bill?

3. Katherine bought a personal diary. The personal diary cost $7.63. Katherine gave the clerk a twenty-dollar bill. How much change did she get?

4. Alexander went to the store and bought a toy car. The toy car cost $10.93. Alexander gave the clerk a ten-dollar bill and a five-dollar bill. How much change did he get?

5. Rob went to the ice cream parlour and had an ice cream sundae. The ice cream sundae cost $5.34. Rob gave the cashier 3 toonies. How much change did he get?

Chalkboard Publishing Inc © 2007   Canadian Money Activities 1-4

Money Problems

A. Solve the following money problems. Show your thinking.

1. How many nickels are in 9 toonies?

2. Bhavin bought a hockey jersey for $54.42. He paid the cashier $60.00. What was his change?

3. How much money in total?
   5 twenty-dollar bills, 6 toonies, 3 loonies, 2 quarters, 5 dimes, 7 nickels and 3 pennies.

4. Sophie bought 5 bunches of lillies. Each bunch cost $4.30. She paid with $20.00. Did she have enough money? Explain.

5. Chris bought 4 music CD's. Each CD cost $15.99. How much did the music CD's cost altogether?

Chalkboard Publishing Inc © 2007

Canadian Money Activities 1-4

Money Problems

A. **S**olve the following money problems. Show your thinking.

1. Valerie bought 5 candy bars for ninety-nine cents each. How much did Valerie spend?

2. A ticket at the movie theatre costs $8.75. Suzanne bought a ticket and also purchased popcorn for $2.40 and a soda for $2.00. How much did Suzanne spend in all?

3. At the market, John purchased 4 apples at 36 cents each. John also purchased 3 oranges for 42 cents. John gave the cashier 2 toonies. What was his change?

4. Kate bought a book for $11.41. Mark bought a book for $16.39. How much more expensive was Mark's book?

5. Amy bought 8 dog treats for $2.34 each. How much did Amy spend?

Chalkboard Publishing Inc © 2007

Canadian Money Activities 1-4

Design Your Own Coin

A. Design your own coin and then write about it.

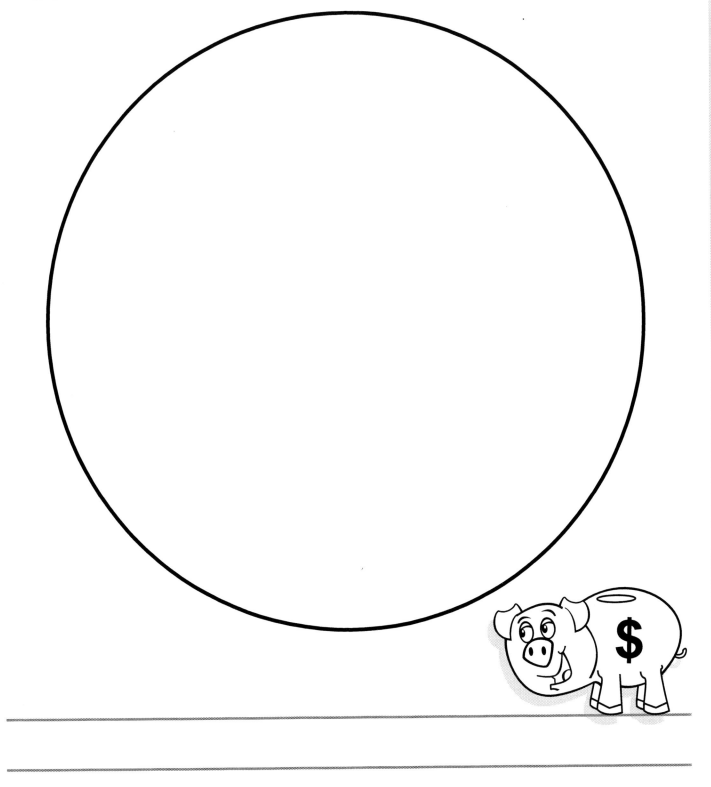

_____

_____

_____

Chalkboard Publishing Inc © 2007

Canadian Money Activities 1-4

Grade 1 Money Test

A. What is the value of each amount of coins?

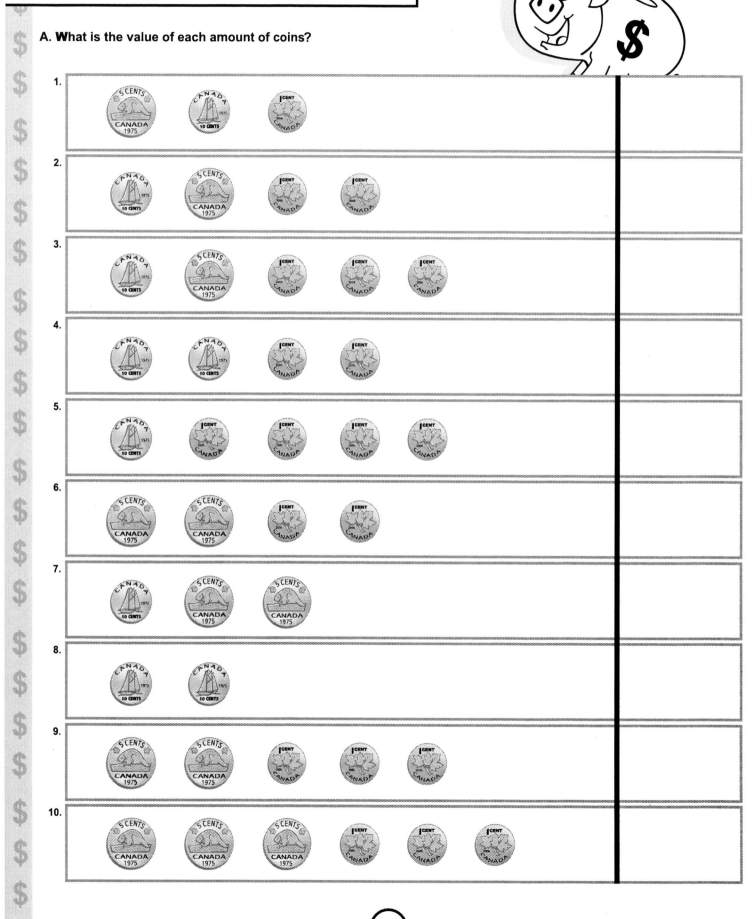

Chalkboard Publishing Inc © 2007

Canadian Money Activities 1-4

Grade 1 Math Test: Coin Addition

A. **Add the coins.**

1.

  + = ___7___ ¢

2.

  +   = ___8___ ¢

3.

   +   = ___5___ ¢

4.

 **+**   = ___9___ ¢

5.

   **+** = ___8___ ¢

Canadian Money Activities 1-4

Grade 1 Math Test: Coin Subtraction

A. **Subtract the coins.**

1.
   ■   = _____ ¢

2.
   ■   = _____ ¢

3.
      = _____ ¢

4.
   = _____ ¢

5.
 ■ = _____ ¢

Chalkboard Publishing Inc © 2007

Canadian Money Activities 1-4

Grade 2 Money Test

A. **W**hat is the value of each amount of coins?

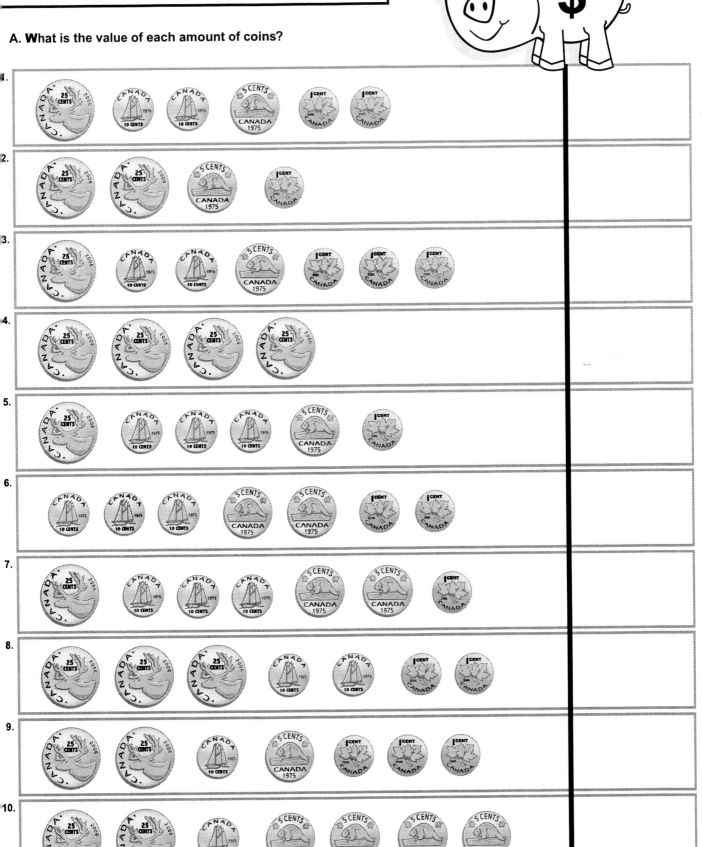

Chalkboard Publishing Inc © 2007

Canadian Money Activities 1-4

Grade 2 Math Test: Coin Addition

A. Add the coins.

	Show your work.

1.  **+** = _____ ¢

2.   **+**  = _____ ¢

3.  **+**  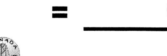 = _____ ¢

4.   **+**   = _____ ¢

5.   **+**   = _____ ¢

Canadian Money Activities 1-4

A. Subtract the coins.

	Show your work.

1.  −  = _____ ¢

2.  −  = _____ ¢

3. 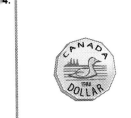 −  = _____ ¢

4.  − = _____ ¢

5.  − = _____ ¢

Grade 3 Money Test

A. What is the value of each amount of money?

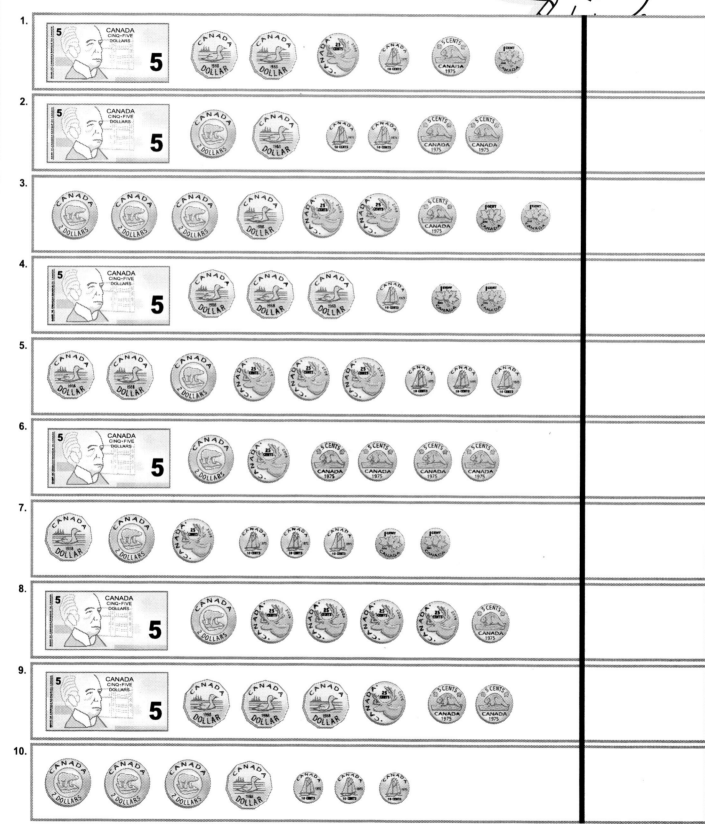

Chalkboard Publishing Inc © 2007

Canadian Money Activities 1-4

Grade 4 Money Test

A. Count and write the value of each amount of money.

1.  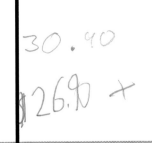 30.40

$26.90 ✗

2.   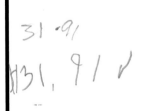 31·91

$31.91 ✓

3.    ✓

$70.46

4.    $117.12

5.     $194.75

Chalkboard Publishing Inc © 2007

Canadian Money Activities 1-4

Grade 3 Money Word Search

A. Find the money words.

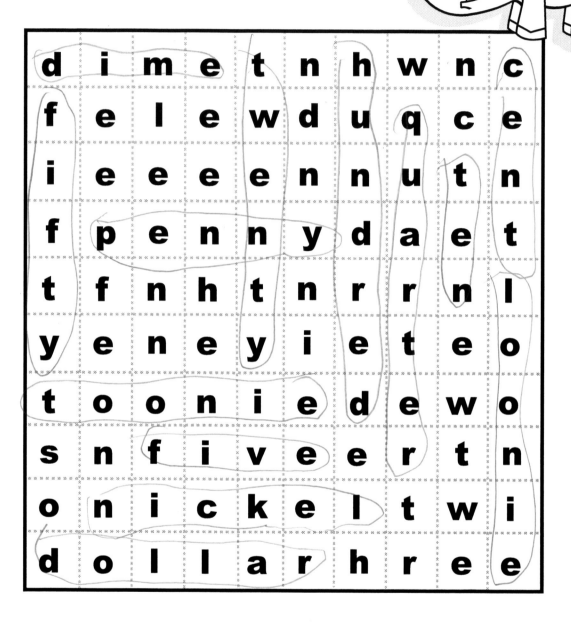

```
d  i  m  e  t  n  h  w  n  c
f  e  l  e  w  d  u  q  c  e
i  e  e  e  n  n  u  t  n
f  p  e  n  n  y  d  a  e  t
t  f  n  h  t  n  r  r  n  l
y  e  n  e  y  i  e  t  e  o
t  o  o  n  i  e  d  e  w  o
s  n  f  i  v  e  e  r  t  n
o  n  i  c  k  e  l  t  w  i
d  o  l  l  a  r  h  r  e  e
```

dollar   cent   nickel   dime   quarter

hundred   loonie   toonie   ten   five

twenty   fifty   penny

Chalkboard Publishing Inc © 2007

Canadian Money Activities 1-4

Adding and Subtracting Money

A. Name: _____   Adding and Subtracting of Money # 1

1. $7.62 - $5.71	2. $5.77 + $1.32	3. $2.60 + $7.79	4. $8.63 - $2.18	5. $6.85 - $2.29	6. $1.82 + $7.31	7. $9.83 - $6.16
8. $5.22 + $3.75	9. $8.75 - $4.37	10. $4.50 - $2.50	11. $7.73 - $5.12	12. $9.85 - $5.12	13. $6.00 + $0.75	14. $9.42 - $1.50
15. $9.23 - $7.19	16. $5.54 + $1.62	17. $1.97 + $4.07	18. $4.31 - $1.80	19. $1.80 + $6.29	20. $2.18 + $7.33	Number Correct: ___ 20

B. Name: _____   Adding and Subtracting of Money # 2

1. $5.73 + $2.36	2. $4.54 + $1.19	3. $6.34 - $3.55	4. $8.16 - $2.35	5. $5.82 + $4.18	6. $8.07 - $4.32	7. $3.00 + $1.56
8. $6.50 - $0.85	9. $9.25 - $3.58	10. $3.42 - $3.35	11. $7.46 - $5.52	12. $7.00 + $0.75	13. $2.25 + $4.80	14. $3.28 - $1.38
15. $2.23 + $4.06	16. $2.81 + $6.62	17. $2.82 + $5.30	18. $4.45 - $1.99	19. $6.75 + $3.48	20. $9.17 - $3.08	Number Correct: ___ 20

Canadian Money Activities 1-4

Adding Money

A. **N**ame: _____   Adding Money # 1

1. $19.73 + $42.32	2. $35.57 + $82.92	3. $23.78 + $32.92	4. $94.61 + $27.95	5. $10.88 + $82.03	6. $40.35 + $45.88	7. $70.57 + $23.50
8. $13.20 + $28.32	9. $82.45 + $55.41	10. $26.66 + $49.12	11. $77.13 + $55.36	12. $80.21 + $13.18	13. $76.23 + $41.92	14. $83.87 + $54.24
15. $21.62 + $40.50	16. $81.61 + $74.12	17. $45.34 + $46.91	18. $91.32 + $84.69	19. $71.24 + $32.99	20. $66.40 + $27.11	

Number Correct:

_____

20

B. **N**ame: _____   Adding Money # 1

1. $11.50 + $73.75	2. $60.91 + $41.67	3. $79.87 + $60.32	4. $26.89 + $99.09	5. $19.48 + $80.07	6. $87.46 + $57.33	7. $52.26 + $77.33
8. $45.41 + $28.37	9. $65.75 + $89.50	10. $96.51 + $87.01	11. $51.65 + $69.54	12. $35.03 + $46.37	13. $27.68 + $60.77	14. $78.25 + $63.77
15. $84.82 + $73.44	16. $60.06 + $70.24	17. $73.59 + $78.20	18. $32.41 + $23.05	19. $82.26 + $69.91	20. $48.57 + $16.70	

Number Correct:

_____

20

Chalkboard Publishing Inc © 2007   **Canadian Money Activities 1-4**

Subtracting Money

1. $13.91 - $13.89	2. $47.16 - $19.78	3. $87.18 - $28.89	4. $53.23 - $14.65	5. $52.75 - $30.66	6. $98.93 - $74.54	7. $41.18 - $12.27
8. $28.36 - $15.98	9. $62.31 - $41.96	10. $44.33 - $42.17	11. $18.83 - $17.79	12. $76.55 - $70.17	13. $14.24 - $12.79	14. $56.74 - $39.49
15. $84.24 - $25.61	16. $82.77 - $15.37	17. $84.05 - $76.28	18. $26.77 - $21.96	19. $17.69 - $17.25	20. $98.92 - $44.08	

Number Correct:

20

1. $59.97 - $57.96	2. $68.41 - $17.01	3. $59.42 - $25.46	4. $17.53 - $16.23	5. $90.91 - $37.04	6. $28.93 - $19.26	7. $43.28 - $29.98
8. $68.72 - $48.83	9. $86.24 - $10.39	10. $26.47 - $14.85	11. $73.97 - $35.46	12. $51.83 - $31.79	13. $54.99 - $30.19	14. $84.12 - $60.38
15. $18.55 - $17.67	16. $86.96 - $38.91	17. $72.92 - $38.43	18. $63.82 - $34.56	19. $76.61 - $27.98	20. $75.27 - $54.24	

Number Correct:

20

Canadian Money Activities 1-4

Canadian Money Flash Cards

This is a penny.

1¢ $0.01

This is a nickel.

5¢ $0.05

This is a dime.

10¢ $0.10

This is a quarter.

25¢ $0.25

This is a loonie.

100¢ $1.00

This is a toonie.

200¢ $2.00

Canadian Money Flash Cards

This is 5 dollars.	This is 10 dollars.

$5.00	$10.00

This is 20 dollars.	This is 50 dollars.

$20.00	$50.00

This is 100 dollars.

$100.00

Chalkboard Publishing Inc © 2007

Making Change

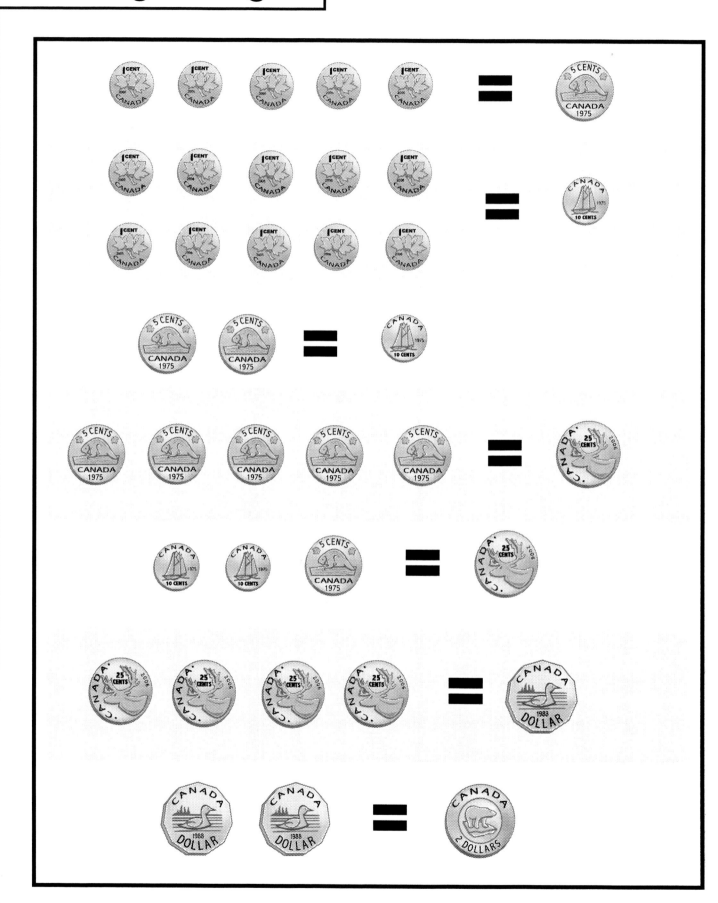

Canadian Money Activities 1-4

Show The Money

. Show the correct amount of money.

1. _____

2. _____

3. _____

4. _____

5. _____

6. _____

Chalkboard Publishing Inc © 2007

Canadian Money Activities 1-4

Show The Money

A. Show the correct amount of money.

1.

2.

3.

4.

5.

Money Masters

Penny

Nickel

Canadian Money Activities 1-4

Money Masters

Dime

Quarter

Chalkboard Publishing Inc © 2007

Canadian Money Activities 1-4

Money Masters

Toonie

Loonie

Canadian Money Activities 1-4

Money Masters

$5.00

$10.00

Canadian Money Activities 1-4

Money Masters

$20.00

$50.00

$100.00

Canadian Money Activities 1-4

Money Concepts Assessment Rubric

$

Student _____

Expectation	Level 1	Level 2	Level 3	Level 4
O identifies coins up to a toonie and states their value				
O represents money amounts up to 20¢ using coin manipulatives				
O represents money amounts up to $1.00 using coin manipulatives				
O represents money amounts up to $10.00 using coin and bill manipulatives				
O represents money amounts up to $100.00 using coin and bill manipulatives				
O adds and subtracts money amounts to 10¢				
O adds and subtracts money amounts to 100¢ using concrete materials, drawings, and symbols				
O adds and subtracts money amounts to 100¢ without concrete materials, drawings, and symbols				
O adds and subtracts money amounts and represents the answer in decimal notation				
O solves money problems				
O solves money problems involving making change				

Place a checkmark on the expectations being assessed.

Teacher Comments:

_____

_____

Level 1- Student rarely applies skills with several errors or omissions.

Level 2 - Student sometimes applies skills with some errors or omissions.

Level 3 - Student usually applies skills with few errors or omissions.

Level 4 - Student consistently applies skills with almost no errors or omissions.

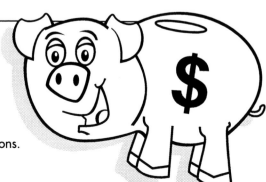

Canadian Money Activities 1-4

WAY TO GO!

You are a money expert!

Name: _____

75

Answer Pages

p2.

A. 1. loonie   B. 7. 10 ¢
2. nickel   8. 25 ¢
3. penny   9. 5 ¢
4. toonie   10. 1 ¢
5. dime
6. quarter

p3.

A. 1. nickel
2. loonie
3. penny
4. toonie
5. dime
6. quarter

p4.

1.   2.   3.

4.   5.   6.

p5.

A. red = 14   B. 1. $0.14
blue = 7   2. $2.50
yellow = 12   3. $0.70
green = 10   4. $0.60

p6.

A. 1. 5 ¢
2. 3 ¢
3. 6 ¢
4. 4 ¢
5. 7 ¢

p7.

A. 1. 25 ¢
2. 15 ¢
3. 30 ¢
4. 20 ¢
5. 35 ¢

p8.

A. 1. 50 ¢
2. 30 ¢
3. 60 ¢
4. 40 ¢
5. 70 ¢

p9.

A. 1. 9 ¢
2. 17 ¢
3. 13 ¢
4. 8 ¢
5. 21 ¢

p10.

A. 1. 55 ¢
2. 50 ¢
3. 65 ¢
4. 45 ¢
5. 60 ¢

p11.

A. 1. 37 ¢
2. 28 ¢
3. 47 ¢
4. 46 ¢
5. 28 ¢

p12.

A. 1. 81 ¢
2. 57 ¢
3. 96 ¢
4. 62 ¢
5. 85 ¢

p13.

A. 1. 17 ¢
2. 13 ¢
3. 12 ¢
4. 20 ¢
5. 9 ¢
6. 18 ¢
7. 16 ¢
8. 12 ¢
9. 20 ¢
10. 19 ¢

p14.

A. 1. 6 ¢
2. 9 ¢
3. 4 ¢
4. 8 ¢
5. 10 ¢

p15.

A. 1. 7 ¢
2. 7 ¢
3. 4 ¢
4. 8 ¢
5. 10 ¢

p16.

A. 1. 8 ¢
2. 5 ¢
3. 3 ¢
4. 6 ¢
5. 4 ¢

p17. Answers may vary.

p18. Answers may vary.

p19.

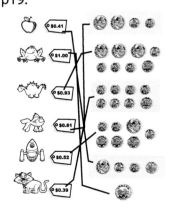

p20. Answers may vary.

Chalkboard Publishing Inc © 2007

Answer Pages

p21. Answers may vary.

p22. Answers may vary.

p23.
A. 1. 87 ¢
   2. 61 ¢
   3. 72 ¢
   4. 87 ¢
   5. 82 ¢

p24.
A. 1. 67 ¢
   2. 67 ¢
   3. 72 ¢
   4. 72 ¢
   5. 86 ¢

p25.
A. 1. 19 ¢
   2. 68 ¢
   3. 58 ¢
   4. 38 ¢
   5. 26 ¢

p26.
A. 1. 54 ¢
   2. 64 ¢
   3. 54 ¢
   4. 18 ¢
   5. 46 ¢

p27.
A. 1. 10 ¢, 10 ¢, 5 ¢, 1 ¢, 1 ¢
   2. 25 ¢, 10 ¢, 5 ¢
   3. 10 ¢, 10 ¢, 1 ¢, 1 ¢, 1 ¢, 1 ¢
   4. 25 ¢, 25 ¢, 25 ¢, 5 ¢, 1 ¢, 1 ¢
   5. 25 ¢, 25 ¢, 10 ¢, 1 ¢,
   6. 5 ¢, 5 ¢, 5 ¢, 1 ¢, 1 ¢, 1 ¢

p28.
A. 1. 25 ¢, 1 ¢, 1 ¢
   2. 25 ¢, 25 ¢, 5 ¢, 1 ¢, 1 ¢, 1 ¢, 1 ¢
   3. 25 ¢, 10 ¢, 10 ¢, 1 ¢, 1 ¢, 1 ¢
   4. 25 ¢, 10 ¢, 1 ¢
   5. 25 ¢, 25 ¢, 10 ¢, 1 ¢, 1 ¢, 1 ¢
   6. 25 ¢, 25 ¢, 25 ¢, 10 ¢, 5 ¢
   7. 25 ¢, 25 ¢, 25 ¢, 10 ¢, 5 ¢, 1 ¢, 1 ¢, 1 ¢, 1 ¢
   8. 25 ¢, 25 ¢, 25 ¢, 5 ¢,
   9. 25 ¢, 10 ¢, 5 ¢, 1 ¢
   6. 25 ¢, 25 ¢, 25 ¢

p29. Answers may vary.

p30. Answers may vary.

p31. Answers may vary.

p32. Answers may vary.

p34.
A. 1. $1, $1,10 ¢, 5 ¢, 5 ¢,
   2. $1, $1, $1, $1, $1, 5 ¢,
      25 ¢, 10 ¢,1 ¢,1 ¢,1 ¢ ,1¢
   3. $2, 25 ¢, 25 ¢, 25 ¢
      5 ¢, 1 ¢,1 ¢,1 ¢,1 ¢
   4. $1, $1, $1, $1, 25 ¢, 25 ¢
      5 ¢,1 ¢ ,1¢
   5. $2, $2, $2, $1, $1, 25 ¢
      25 ¢, 25 ¢,5 ¢,1 ¢,1 ¢

p33.
A. 1. 69 ¢
   2. 7 pennies
   3. 10 nickels
   4. 1 quarter
   5. 2 quarters
   6. 0 pennies
   7. 7 pennies
   8. 75 ¢

p35. Answers may vary.
A. 1. 79 ¢ = 25 ¢, 25 ¢, 25 ¢, 1 ¢, 1 ¢, 1 ¢, 1 ¢
   2. 77 ¢ = 25 ¢, 25 ¢, 10 ¢, 10 ¢, 5 ¢, 1 ¢, 1 ¢
   3. 98 ¢ = 25 ¢, 25 ¢, 25 ¢, 10 ¢, 10 ¢, 1 ¢, 1 ¢, 1 ¢
   4. 92 ¢ = 25 ¢, 25 ¢, 25 ¢, 10 ¢, 5 ¢, 1 ¢, 1 ¢
   5. 54 ¢ = 25 ¢, 25 ¢, 1 ¢, 1 ¢, 1 ¢, 1 ¢
   6. 48 ¢ = 25 ¢, 10 ¢, 10 ¢, 1 ¢, 1 ¢, 1 ¢

Canadian Money Activities 1-4

Answer Pages

p37.
A. 1. $0.85, $0.85, $0.90, $0.95, $1.15, $1.50, $1.80, $1.90
   2. $4.15
   3. $3.55
   4. $0.10
   5. $2.65, yes, he still has $1.35 to spend.

p38.
A. 1. $3.20, no, Jane needs $0.20 more.
   2. Answers may vary.
   3. yes, Michael has $1.15 left
   4. Answers may vary.
   5. Answers may vary.

p39.
A. 1. $7.08, > $5.52
   2. $7.90, > $7.67
   3. $21.51, = $21.51

B. 7. $12.09
   8. $44.06
   9. $9.44

p40.
A. 1. $24.08, > $13.57
   2. $5.20, < $7.67
   3. $8.05, < $9.55
   4. $8.35, > $7.32
   5. $9.80, < $10.71

p41.
A. 1. $20.27
   2. $73.00
   3. $102.58
   4. $71.30
   5. $54.52

p42.
A. 1. $53.85
   2. $71.61
   3. $69.71
   4. $103.24
   5. $36.67

p43.
A. 1. $40.32
   2. $21.55
   3. $30.75
   4. $0.54
   5. $5.78
   6. $0.53
   7. $24.45
   8. $0.16
   9. $2.40
   10. $1.65
   11. $11.60
   12. $11.95
   13. $30.75
   14. $2.97
   15. $16.03

p44.
A. 1. $1.98
   2. $62.31
   3. $80.95
   4. $42.73
   5. $10.91
   6. $1.22
   7. $50.85
   8. $11.62
   9. $30.84
   10. $0.61
   11. $0.80
   12. $19.25
   13. $5.65
   14. $1.17
   15. $70.40

p45.
A. 1. $929.00
   2. $6.00
   3. $70.00
   4. $10.00
   5. $6.00
   6. $170.00
   7. $8.00
   8. $407.00
   9. $639.00
   10. $79.00
   11. $74.00
   12. $3.00
   13. $612.00
   14. $7.00
   15. $85.00
   16. $91.00
   17. $578.00
   18. $7.00

p46 .
A. 1. $100.00
   2. $50.00
   3. $2.00
   4. $5.00
   5. $2.00
   6. $37.00
   7. $10.00
   8. $50.00
   9. $30.00
   10. $7.00
   11. $4.00
   12. $40.00
   13. $7.00
   14. $35.00
   15. $31.00
   16. $8.00
   17. $7.00
   18. $3.00

p47 .

$53.82	>	$3.82	$78.25	>	$25.78
$0.97	=	$0.97	$34.59	>	$26.59
$61.18	<	$80.04	$5.35	<	$5.76
$36.50	>	$35.60	$2.31	<	$2.57
$59.43	<	$59.44	$8.01	<	$8.10
$43.05	>	$12.82	$6.80	>	$6.44
$4.76	<	$9.99	$94.53	<	$94.60
$87.27	<	$87.72	$7.16	<	$7.61
$2.43	>	$1.38	$56.74	>	$56.06

p48.
A. 1. $13.42
   2. $6.16
   3. $12.37
   4. $4.07
   5. $0.66

p49.
A. 1. 360
   2. $5.58
   3. $116.38
   4. No change. She owes $1.50
   5. $63.96

Chalkboard Publishing Inc © 2007

Canadian Money Activities 1-4

Answer Pages

p50.
A. 1. $4.95
2. $13.15
3. $1.30
4. $4.98
5. $18.72

p51. Answers may vary.

p52.
A. 1. $0.16
2. $0.17
3. $0.18
4. $0.22
5. $0.14
6. $0.12
7. $0.20
8. $0.20
9. $0.13
10. $0.18

p53.
A. 1. 7 ¢
2. 8 ¢
3. 5 ¢
4. 9 ¢
5. 8 ¢

p54.
A. 1. 4 ¢
2. 7 ¢
3. 2 ¢
4. 7 ¢
5. 4 ¢

p55.
A. 1. 52 ¢
2. 56 ¢
3. 53 ¢
4. $1.00 or loonie
5. 61 ¢
6. 42 ¢
7. 66 ¢
8. 97 ¢
9. 68 ¢
10. 80 ¢

p56.
A. 1. 52 ¢
2. 82 ¢
3. 71 ¢
4. 91 ¢
5. 77 ¢

p57.
A. 1. 44 ¢
2. 63 ¢
3. 58 ¢
4. 48 ¢
5. 46 ¢

p58.
A. 1. $7.41
2. $8.30
3. $7.57
4. $8.12
5. $5.05
6. $7.45
7. $3.57
8. $8.05
9. $8.35
10. $7.30

p59.
A. 1. $30.40
2. $31.91
3. $70.36
4. $117.12
5. $94.75

p60.

d	i	m	e	t	n	h	w	n	c
f	e	l	e	w	d	u	q	c	e
i	e	e	e	e	n	n	u	t	n
f	p	e	n	n	y	d	a	e	t
t	f	n	h	t	n	r	r	n	l
y	e	n	e	y	i	e	t	e	o
t	o	o	n	i	e	d	e	w	o
s	n	f	i	v	e	e	r	t	n
o	n	i	c	k	e	l	t	w	i
d	o	l	l	a	r	h	r	e	e

p61.

A. 1. $1.91
2. $7.09
3. $10.39
4. $6.45
5. $4.56
6. $9.13
7. $3.67
8. $8.97
9. $4.38
10. $2.00
11. $2.61
12. $4.73
13. $6.75
14. $7.92
15. $2.04
16. $7.16
17. $6.04
18. $2.51
19. $8.09
20. $9.51

B. 1. $8.09
2. $5.73
3. $2.79
4. $5.81
5. $10.00
6. $3.75
7. $4.56
8. $5.65
9. $5.67
10. $0.07
11. $1.94
12. $7.75
13. $7.05
14. $1.90
15. $6.29
16. $9.43
17. $8.12
18. $2.46
19. $10.23
20. $6.09

p62.

	A.			B.	
	1.	$62.05		1.	$85.25
	2.	$118.49		2.	$102.58
	3.	$56.70		3.	$140.19
	4.	$122.56		4.	$125.98
	5.	$92.91		5.	$99.55
	6.	$86.23		6.	$144.79
	7.	$94.07		7.	$129.59
	8.	$41.52		8.	$73.78
	9.	$137.86		9.	$155.25
	10.	$75.78		10.	$183.52
	11.	$132.49		11.	$121.19
	12.	$93.39		12.	$81.40
	13.	$118.15		13.	$88.45
	14.	$138.11		14.	$142.02
	15.	$62.12		15.	$158.26
	16.	$155.73		16.	$130.30
	17.	$92.25		17.	$151.79
	18.	$176.01		18.	$55.46
	19.	$104.23		19.	$152.17
	20.	$93.51		20.	$65.27

p63.

	A.			B.	
	1.	$0.02		1.	$2.01
	2.	$27.38		2.	$51.40
	3.	$58.29		3.	$33.96
	4.	$38.58		4.	$1.30
	5.	$22.09		5.	$53.87
	6.	$24.39		6.	$9.67
	7.	$28.91		7.	$13.30
	8.	$12.38		8.	$19.89
	9.	$20.35		9.	$75.85
	10.	$2.16		10.	$11.62
	11.	$1.04		11.	$38.51
	12.	$6.38		12.	$20.04
	13.	$1.45		13.	$24.80
	14.	$17.25		14.	$23.74
	15.	$58.63		15.	$0.88
	16.	$67.40		16.	$48.05
	17.	$7.77		17.	$34.49
	18.	$4.81		18.	$29.26
	19.	$0.44		19.	$48.63
	20.	$54.84		20.	$21.03

Canadian Money Activities 1-4